I Will Trust in Heavenly Father and His Son, Jesus Christ

Sharing Time Activities

Written and Illustrated by Shauna Mooney Kawasaki

DESERET BOOK

SALT LAKE CITY, UTAH

© 2005 Shauna Mooney Kawasaki

All rights reserved. Individual illustrations may be reproduced for use in the classroom or at home. Whenever possible, please include a credit line indicating the title, author, and publisher. For other use of this book or any part herein, please contact the publisher, Deseret Book Company, P. O. Box 30178, Salt Lake City, Utah 84130. This work is not an official publication of The Church of Jesus Christ of Latter-day Saints. The views expressed herein are the responsibility of the author and do not necessarily represent the position of the Church or of Deseret Book Company.

DESERET BOOK is a registered trademark of Deseret Book Company.

Visit us at deseretbook.com

ISBN 1-59038-492-X

Printed in the United States of America   77894
Seagull Press, Salt Lake City, Utah

10   9   8   7   6   5   4   3   2   1

Introduction

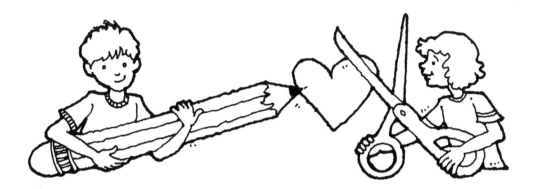

Jesus said, "For I will fulfil my promises which I have made unto the children of men" (2 Nephi 10:17). During the year 2006, and for many years to come, children of our Heavenly Father will learn about the promises made to them and the blessings they can receive when they follow him in faith, listen to his Spirit, and learn of him. Heavenly Father and his son Jesus Christ love us, know us, and will always keep their promises. They have given us the gospel, the scriptures, and latter-day prophets to guide us. Above all, Heavenly Father has given us a plan of happiness, with Jesus Christ as our promised Savior.

This book is designed to help Primary presidencies, teachers, and parents follow the 2006 sharing time outline and monthly themes set forth by the Primary General Board. Each of the twelve chapters correlates with one of the twelve areas of focus for the year. All of the activities are designed to be used in a variety of settings, including sharing time, class time, personal time, and in family home evening lessons. The activities can be adjusted for group or individual use, as well as for use with either senior or junior Primary groups or for Activity Days girls. For younger children, select just one element from the activity you want to use.

At the beginning of each chapter is a scripture study chart. Make a copy for each child to take home so that scripture study can be recorded and a habit made of it.

Photocopying, coloring, cutting, laminating, and employing your own creativity are encouraged as you use all of the activities in this book to enhance your lessons, sharing time presentations, and family home evenings.

The CD-ROM that accompanies this book contains all of the artwork (in PDF format) for the activities in this book. The artwork is listed on the CD-ROM by page number and is ready to print. To use it:

1. Put the CD-ROM face up in your computer's CD-ROM drive.

2. Go to your computer's "desktop" and double-click the icon labeled My Computer.

3. Navigate to the CD-ROM and double-click it. A window will open showing the files on the CD-ROM.

4. Double-click the icon for the page number of the artwork you want to print. The artwork should open in Adobe's Acrobat Reader program. If it doesn't, and your computer asks you to select a program to open the file, you'll need to download and install Adobe's free Acrobat Reader. You can download the program here:

http://www.adobe.com/products/acrobat/readstep2_allversions.html

5. Print the artwork by clicking File > Print. (To print a larger or smaller version, change the scale in File > Page Setup first.)

Feel free to use your creativity in adapting any of the ideas and concepts in this book. It is hoped that you will find them a valuable resource in your important work of helping children learn about Heavenly Father's plan for them.

JANUARY

The Promises of Heavenly Father and Jesus Christ Are Recorded in the Scriptures

Heavenly Father and Jesus Christ have made many promises to us. These promises are recorded in the scriptures. When prophets or apostles speak or write by the power of the Holy Ghost, their words become scripture. Doctrine and Covenants 68:4 says: "And whatsoever they shall speak when moved upon by the Holy Ghost shall be scripture." The Standard Works, or official scriptures of the Church, are the Bible, the Book of Mormon, the Doctrine and Covenants, and the Pearl of Great Price. We are blessed with these holy books so that we can read of the promises Heavenly Father and Jesus Christ have made to us, how these promises are kept, and how they will bless all of us if we are faithful.

Jesus Christ is our light. Through scripture study we can find that light and apply it to our lives. When we read, study, and obey the scriptures, the Lord will keep his promises (see Alma 37:17).

Color in one space for each day of the month that you read your scriptures.
Use the chart on the right to determine what color to use each day.

WHAT GIVES LIGHT?

Color the pictures that give us light; cross out the pictures that don't give light. Which item can give us spiritual light?

"CHRIST SHALL GIVE THEE LIGHT."
EPHESIANS 5:14

Read Ether chapters 1 through 6. Help the Jaredites on their journey by numbering the verses in order beginning with Ether 1:38. Use the numbers 1 through 22.

COMMANDMENTS ARE TRUE

After reading each scripture, choose one of the letters below to help finish the word that describes how to keep Heavenly Father's commandments.

	_LEDGES D&C 136:20
	_ECEIVE MATTHEW 18:5
	_ATH D&C 84:40
	_AKE A PROMISE ALMA 37:17
	_NTEGRITY JOB 27:5
	_WEAR 3 NEPHI 3:8
	_TERNAL ALMA 37:44

M P O R E I S

FEBRUARY

Heavenly Father's Plan Promises Eternal Happiness

When we turn eight years old, we can be baptized and receive the gift of the Holy Ghost. We can start walking the path that leads to eternal life. In Moses 1:39, the Lord declared, "This is my work and my glory—to bring to pass the immortality and eternal life of man." Through the atonement of Jesus Christ, everyone can receive this promised gift.

Heavenly Father wants us to live as Jesus taught; he wants us to choose the right, repent when necessary, and return to live with him. If we are obedient and faithful, we can be happy, peaceful, and secure, just as if we were wearing the armor of God described in Ephesians 6. With this armor, we can "press forward with a steadfastness in Christ, having a perfect brightness of hope, and a love of God and of all men. Wherefore, if ye . . . endure to the end, behold, thus saith the Father: Ye shall have eternal life" (2 Nephi 31:20).

Read your scriptures every day and color in the corresponding number on the picture. After 28 days, the picture will be complete.

IMPORTANT & Not-So-

We make many choices every day. Some are more important than others. Color and cut out the pictures. Divide them into groups of "important" and "not so important" choices.

IMPORTANT CHOICES

Talk about how your choices can help you follow Heavenly Father's plan.

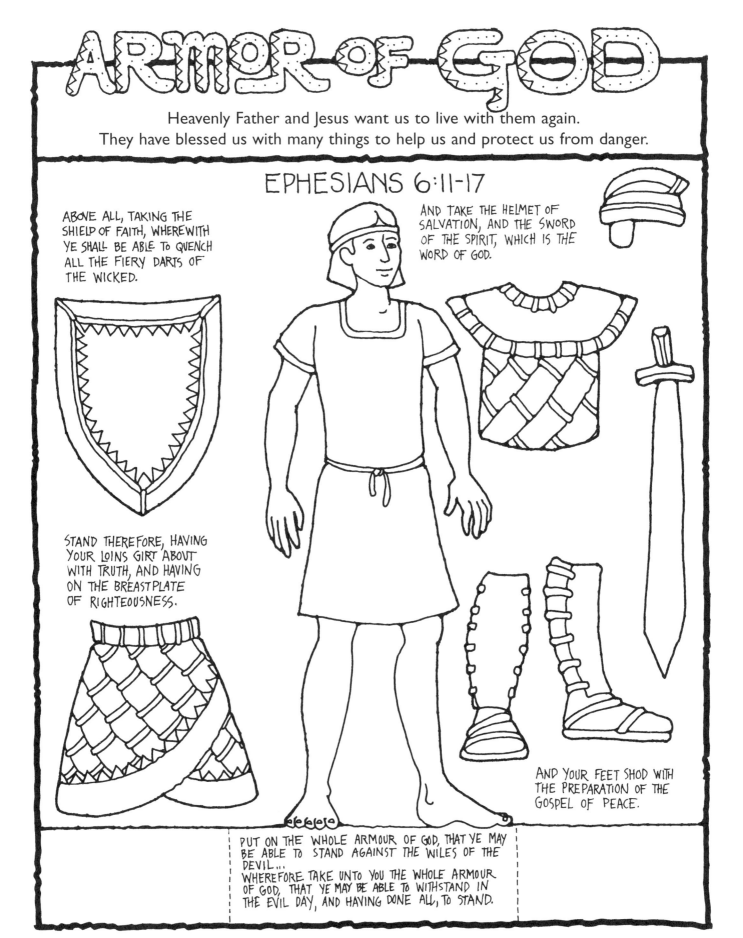

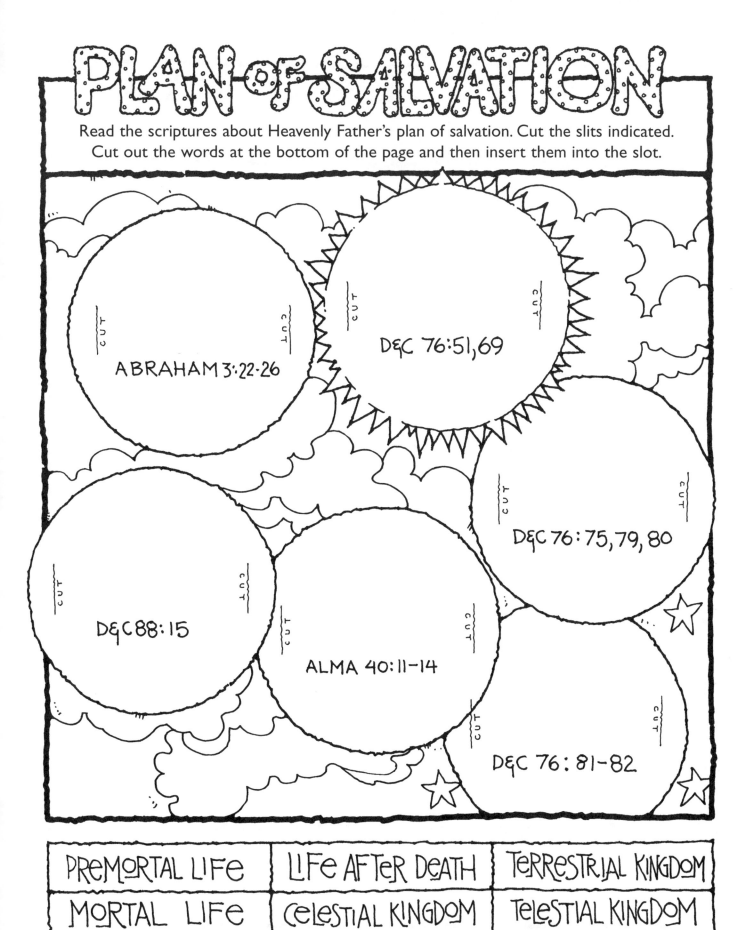

MARCH

Heavenly Father and Jesus Christ Make Promises through the Prophets

As members of The Church of Jesus Christ of Latter-day Saints, we are blessed to be led by living prophets. These are men inspired to speak for the Lord, just as Moses, Nephi, and many other prophets of old did. Prophets tell us what Heavenly Father wants us to do, and what Jesus Christ has taught us and promised us. If we listen to their messages, we will learn how Father in Heaven loves us and what he wants us to do.

"What I the Lord have spoken, I have spoken, and I excuse not myself; and though the heavens and the earth pass away, my word shall not pass away, but shall all be fulfilled, whether by mine own voice or by the voice of my servants, it is the same" (D&C 1:38). Like prophets of old, the prophets today testify of the gospel of Jesus Christ.

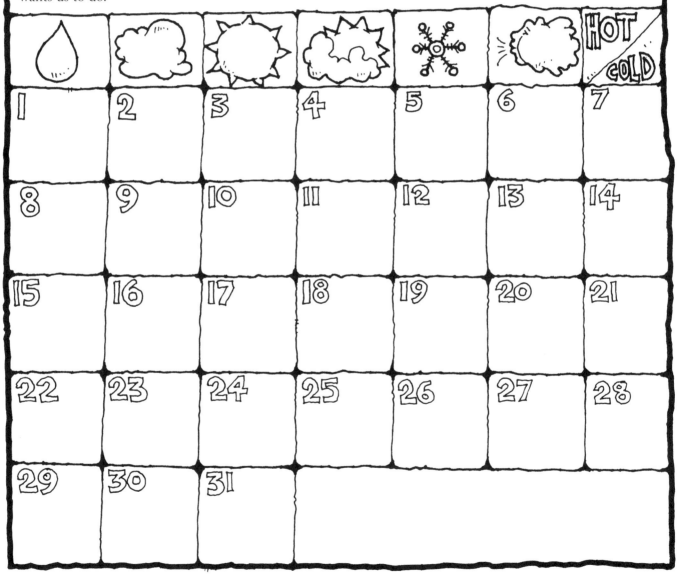

As you read the scriptures each day, draw the weather symbol on the corresponding date to keep track of the weather changes in March.

Draw and color a picture of your family inside the frame.
Decorate the frame. Be sure to sign and date the picture and keep it in your journal.

PROPHETS

Color and cut out each prophet card. Read more about each prophet in the Bible Dictionary or Index.

14

Write what you learn on the back of each card. Punch a hole in the left-hand corner and tie with yarn to make a flip chart.

PROPHETS TODAY

Look up, down, across, and diagonally to find the words in the chart below.
Cross off each word as you find it. Read about prophets in the Bible Dictionary.

```
F D G B Z J F T H E H K N P G
C I P H C A S W Q U O R U M J
F I R S T P R E S I D E N C Y
Q H E S R O F L G E M J B F L
U P S Q T S R V S E V E N T Y
O W I U K T H E L T H E S D T
R M D O F L N Q S E V E N T Y
U V E P R E S I D I N G C T X
M T N B I S H O P R I C O K Y
S E C O N D N F T H E W F L F
T S Y M R Q U O R U M D B P Q
```

- FIRST PRESIDENCY
- QUORUM OF THE TWELVE APOSTLES
- PRESIDENCY OF THE SEVENTY
- FIRST QUORUM OF THE SEVENTY
- SECOND QUORUM OF THE SEVENTY
- PRESIDING BISHOPRIC

APRIL

Heavenly Father Loves Me, So He Sent His Son, the Promised Messiah

In the Grand Council in Heaven, Heavenly Father chose Jesus Christ to be our Savior and to fulfill his promise to us of eternal happiness. In that Grand Council, one plan was presented. Jesus Christ sustained Heavenly Father's plan, which would give us agency to choose for ourselves; but Lucifer attempted to change that plan. We chose to follow the Savior and come to this earth, receive a body, and learn to make choices. If we make wrong choices, Jesus Christ has provided a way for us to repent and return to him.

We can do many things for ourselves, such as eat, drink, dress ourselves, and so on. But what Jesus did for us we cannot do. He was foreordained to carry out the Atonement—to come to earth, suffer the penalty for our sins, die on the cross, and be resurrected. Jesus was resurrected so that we may live again. The third article of faith states, "We believe that through the Atonement of Christ, all mankind may be saved, by obedience to the laws and ordinances of the Gospel."

On the next day much people that were come to the feast, when they heard that Jesus was coming to Jerusalem, took branches of palm trees, and went forth to meet him, and cried, Hosanna: Blessed is the King of Israel that cometh in the name of the Lord. John 12:12–13

Color in one palm branch for each day you read the scriptures this month. You should reach the gates of Jerusalem by the end of the month if you read every day.

REPENTANCE

Agency is the freedom to choose. By using our agency and choosing correctly, we can learn to be more like our Heavenly Father.

	GE OF ACCOUNTABILITY	G
	RAND COUNCIL IN HEAVEN	A
	TERNAL LIFE	E
	OTICE THE SPIRIT IS NEAR	Y
	HOOSE THE RIGHT	C
	OU ARE FREE TO CHOOSE	N

Cut out the letters on the right and glue them in the correct spaces on the left as you discuss the principles of agency, choice and accountability, and repentance.

Use the code to fill in the letters and words of the third article of faith. When you are finished, write your feelings about this article of faith on the lines below.

We believe that through the Atonement of Christ, all mankind may be saved, by obedience to the laws and ordinances of the Gospel.

We can do many things for and by ourselves. But Jesus did something for us that we could never do. He atoned for our sins.

Color the page and then read Alma 34:14–15.
Write down your feelings about Jesus' atonement.

MAY

Heavenly Father Gave Me the Gospel of Jesus Christ. It Was Promised before the World.

When Jesus Christ was on the earth, he established his church among his followers. After his crucifixion and his apostles' deaths, the fulness of the gospel was taken from the earth because of apostasy. Through Joseph Smith, Heavenly Father restored the gospel. The gospel is Heavenly Father's plan of happiness. In its fulness, the gospel includes all of the doctrines, principles, laws, ordinances, and covenants necessary for us to live forever with our Father in Heaven.

Without the Savior and his teachings, there would be no fulness of truth or priesthood authority. As members of The Church of Jesus Christ of Latter-day Saints, we can receive the blessings that were absent from the earth for almost two thousand years and receive strength from the promise that the Church will one day "fill the whole earth" (D&C 109:72; see also Daniel 2:35).

Mothers have many tasks and jobs. Remember your mother as you read the scriptures every day this month. After each day of reading, color one of the objects above. Each object represents something moms do to take care of their families.

JOSEPH SMITH TIME LINE

① **1805** JOSEPH SMITH JR. IS BORN IN VERMONT.

② **1816** JOSEPH SMITH SR. MOVES HIS FAMILY TO PALMYRA, NEW YORK.

③ **1820** AFTER STUDYING JAMES 1:5, 14-YEAR-OLD JOSEPH PRAYS AND IS VISITED BY HEAVENLY FATHER AND JESUS.

④ **1823** ANGEL MORONI VISITS JOSEPH FOUR TIMES.

⑤ **1827** JOSEPH WORKS FOR JOSIAH STOAL AND MEETS EMMA HALE. THEY MARRY.

⑥ **1829** JOSEPH COMPLETES THE TRANSLATION OF THE BOOK OF MORMON WITH THE HELP OF OLIVER COWDERY.

⑦ **1829** MAY 15, JOHN THE BAPTIST RESTORES THE AARONIC PRIESTHOOD.

⑧ **1829** THREE WITNESSES—OLIVER COWDERY, DAVID WHITMER, AND MARTIN HARRIS—SEE THE GOLD PLATES.

⑨ **1829** PETER, JAMES, AND JOHN RESTORE THE MELCHIZEDEK PRIESTHOOD.

⑩ **1830** THE BOOK OF MORMON IS PRINTED AND GOES ON SALE IN PALMYRA.

⑪ **1830** IN JUNE, THE FIRST GENERAL CONFERENCE IS HELD.

⑫ **1830** THE CALL GOES OUT FOR MISSIONARIES TO GO TEACH THE LAMANITES.

⑬ **1830** APRIL 6, THE CHURCH IS ORGANIZED IN THE HOME OF PETER WHITMER SR. IN FAYETTE, NEW YORK.

⑭ **1831** JOSEPH SMITH ARRIVES IN KIRTLAND, OHIO.

⑮ **1831** IN AUGUST, THE PROPHET DEDICATES THE TEMPLE SITE IN INDEPENDENCE, MISSOURI.

⑯ **1832** THE "OLIVE LEAF" REVELATION (D&C 88) IS RECEIVED, CALLING FOR THE CONSTRUCTION OF A TEMPLE IN KIRTLAND, OHIO.

⑰ **1833** REVELATION GIVEN TO THE PROPHET ON THE WORD OF WISDOM.

⑱ **1833** THE SAINTS ARE EXPELLED FROM JACKSON COUNTY.

⑲ **1835** JOSEPH SMITH BUYS MUMMIES AND PAPYRI ROLLS. TRANSLATES THE BOOK OF ABRAHAM FROM THEM.

⑳ **1835** THE DOCTRINE AND COVENANTS IS ACCEPTED AS SCRIPTURE.

㉑ **1835** EMMA SMITH'S HYMNAL IS PUBLISHED.

㉒ **1836** THE KIRTLAND TEMPLE IS DEDICATED.

㉓ **1836** APRIL 3, JESUS APPEARS IN THE TEMPLE. MOSES, ELIAS, AND ELIJAH APPEAR AND GIVE PRIESTHOOD KEYS.

㉔ **1837** THE FIRST MISSIONARIES PREACH IN GREAT BRITAIN.

㉕ **1838** OUR CHURCH'S NAME IS REVEALED. THE CHURCH OF JESUS CHRIST OF LATTER-DAY SAINTS.

㉖ **1838** THE PROPHET AND OTHER CHURCH LEADERS ARE ARRESTED AND PUT ON TRIAL. LATER THEY ARE PUT IN JAIL.

㉗ **1839** JOSEPH SMITH ESTABLISHES NAUVOO FOR THE GATHERING OF THE SAINTS.

㉘ **1840** NAUVOO TEMPLE CONSTRUCTION BEGINS.

㉙ **1840** JOSEPH SMITH TEACHES ABOUT BAPTISM FOR THE DEAD.

㉚ **1841** NAUVOO TEMPLE BAPTISMAL FONT IS DEDICATED.

㉛ **1842** JOSEPH SMITH ORGANIZES THE RELIEF SOCIETY.

㉜ **1842** JOSEPH SMITH ADMINISTERS THE ENDOWMENT TO NINE FAITHFUL BRETHREN.

㉝ **1842** WENTWORTH LETTER (ARTICLES OF FAITH) AND BOOK OF ABRAHAM ARE PUBLISHED IN *TIMES AND SEASONS*.

㉞ **1843** MISSIONARIES ARE CALLED TO SERVE IN THE PACIFIC.

㉟ **1844** THE PROPHET IS NOMINATED TO RUN FOR PRESIDENT OF THE UNITED STATES.

㊱ **1844** ON JUNE 27, JOSEPH SMITH IS MARTYRED AT CARTHAGE JAIL ALONG WITH HIS BROTHER HYRUM.

Cut out the thirty-six strips that describe events in the Prophet Joseph Smith's life.
Cut out the large rectangle at the top of the page and fold it in half on the dotted line.
Tape the edges together to make a pocket to hold the event strips.

HOLDING HANDS

The fulness of the gospel will one day cover the world.
Color the picture of the world. Color and cut out the pictures of the children.

Link their arms together to make a chain of children holding hands around the world.

Color and cut out the standard works. Write your favorite scriptures from these books on the back and keep them in your scriptures.

BOOK OF MORMON

DOCTRINE AND COVENANTS

PEARL OF GREAT PRICE

OLD TESTAMENT

NEW TESTAMENT

JUNE

Heavenly Father and Jesus Christ Promise Me Blessings When I Obey the Commandments

One of our responsibilities on this earth is to show Heavenly Father our willingness to obey his commandments. True freedom comes only from following Jesus' example and keeping the commandments. Heavenly Father gave us loving instructions for our happiness and our physical and spiritual well-being.

We are given commandments in different ways and forms. We received the Ten Commandments through Moses. We were blessed with the Beatitudes from the teachings of Jesus Christ. Our current leaders have given us the guidelines outlined in "My Gospel Standards" to help us in these troubled times. Other commandments have come through latter-day revelation. Our obedience to the commandments is an expression of our love for Heavenly Father and Jesus Christ.

Fathers have many tasks and jobs. Remember your father as you read the scriptures every day this month. After each day of reading, color one of the objects above. Each object represents something dads do to take care of their families.

10 Commandments

Replace each symbol with the letter it represents to reveal the Ten Commandments.
Write your answers on a separate piece of paper.

EXODUS 20:3-17

And God spake all these words,

1 Thou shalt have no other gods before me.

2 Thou shalt not make unto thee any graven image, or any likeness of any thing that is in heaven above, or that is in the water under the earth: thou shalt not bow down thyself to them, nor serve them: for I the Lord thy God am a jealous God,...

3 Thou shalt not take the name of the Lord thy God in vain; for the Lord will not hold him guiltless that taketh his name in vain.

4 Remember the sabbath day, to keep it holy. Six days shalt thou labour, and do all thy work: but the seventh day is the sabbath of the Lord thy God: in it thou shalt not do any work... for in six days the Lord made heaven and earth, the sea, and all that in them is, and rested the seventh day: wherefore the Lord blessed the sabbath day, and hallowed it.

5 Honour thy father and thy mother: that thy days may be long upon the land which the Lord thy God giveth thee.

6 Thou shalt not kill.

7 Thou shalt not commit adultery.

8 Thou shalt not steal.

9 Thou shalt not bear false witness against thy neighbour.

10 Thou shalt not covet thy neighbour's house... nor any thing that is thy neighbour's.

T-■ L-▲ R-▲ S-● H-■

THE BEATITUDES

Replace each symbol with the letter it represents to reveal the Beatitudes Jesus presented on the Sermon on the Mount. Check your answers by reading Matthew 5:3–11.

BL★SS★D ■R★ TH★ P♥♥R •N SP•R•T: F♥R TH★●RS •S TH★ K•NGD♥M ♥F H■■V■N.

BL★SS★D ■R★ TH★Y TH■T M♥■RN: F♥R TH★Y SH■LL B★ C♥MF♥RT★D.

BL★SS★D ■R★ TH★ M■★K: F♥R TH★Y SH■LL •NH★R•T TH★ ★■RTH.

BL★SS★D ■R★ TH★Y WH•CH D♥ H■NG★R ■ND TH•RST ■FT★R R•GHT★♥■SN★SS: F♥R TH★Y SH■LL B★ F•LL★D.

BL★SS★D ■R★ TH★ M★RC•F■L: F♥R TH★Y SH■LL ♥BT■•N M★RCY.

BL★SS★D ■R★ TH★ P■R★ •N H★■RT: F♥R TH★Y SH■LL S★★ G♥D.

BL★SS★D ■R★ TH★ P★■C■M■K★RS: F♥R TH★Y SH■LL B★ C■LL★D TH★ CH•LDR★N ♥F G♥D.

BL★SS★D ■R★ TH★Y WH•CH ■R★ P★RS★CAT★D F♥R R•GHT★♥■SN★SS' S■K★: F♥R TH★●RS •S TH★ K•NGD♥M ♥F H■■V■N.

BL★SS★D ■R★ Y★ WH★N M■N SH■LL R★V•L★ Y♥U, ■ND P★RS★CUT★ Y♥▲, ■ND SH■LL S■Y ■LL M■NN★R ♥F ★V•L ■G■•NST Y♥▲ F■LS★LY, F♥R MY S■K★.

| A-■ | E-★ | I-• | O-♥ | U-▲ |

MY GOSPEL STANDARDS

Replace each symbol with the letter it represents to reveal the statements of "My Gospel Standards." Match each statement to an illustration on pages 54–55.

I will remember my baptismal covenants and listen to the Holy Ghost.

I will be honest with Heavenly Father, others, and myself.

I will seek good friends and treat others kindly.

I will dress modestly to show respect for Heavenly Father and myself.

I will only read and watch things that are pleasing to Heavenly Father.

I will only listen to music that is pleasing to Heavenly Father.

I will use the names of Heavenly Father and Jesus reverently. I will not swear or use crude words.

I will keep my mind and body sacred and pure, and I will not partake of things that are harmful to me.

I will do those things on the Sabbath that will help me feel close to Heavenly Father.

I will choose the right. I know I can repent when I make a mistake.

I will live now to be worthy to go to the temple and serve a mission. I will follow Heavenly Father's plan for me.

| R-C | M-▲ | T-▮ | N-D | S-● |

KEEP THE COMMANDMENTS

Cut out the squares on the solid lines. Following the diagram, weave the two squares together to find out what we need to do about the commandments.

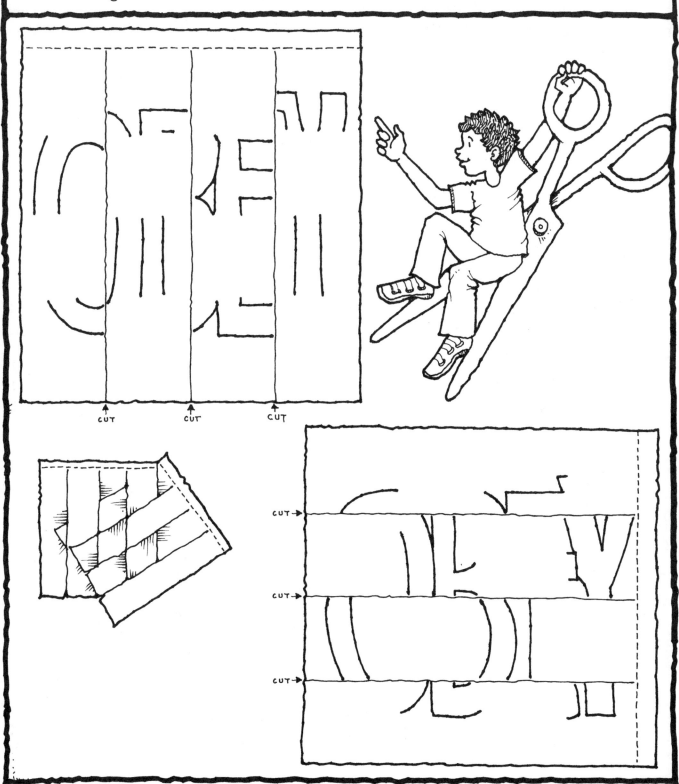

JULY

Heavenly Father Promises to Hear My Prayers and Answer Them

Our Heavenly Father heard the prayers of his children in ancient times; he heard the prayers of the pioneers crossing the plains; and he hears the prayers of the children on the earth today.

Our Father in Heaven loves us and knows of our needs. He wants us to communicate with him through prayer. By praying often and sincerely, we will come to know him, and our desires will become more like his. The power of our prayers depends on us. We need to make our prayers meaningful. We need to use language that shows love, reverence, and respect. We must always give thanks to our Heavenly Father, who has given us everything. We must seek his guidance and strength in all we do and remember the needs of others as we pray. We should seek the guidance of the Holy Ghost and do all we can to help our requests to be granted. As we continue to pray and learn to know our Father in Heaven, we will recognize his wise answers.

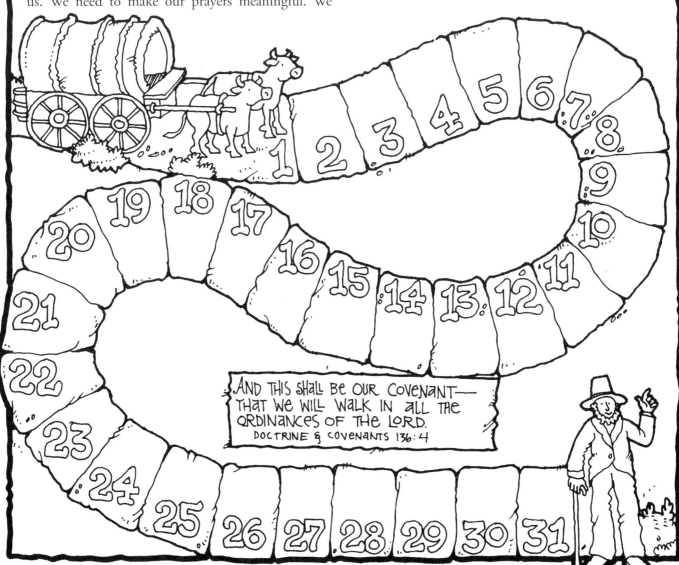

AND THIS SHALL BE OUR COVENANT—THAT WE WILL WALK IN ALL THE ORDINANCES OF THE LORD.
DOCTRINE & COVENANTS 136:4

Read your scriptures every day. Starting at the covered wagon, color in one space every day you read your scriptures until you reach Brigham Young in Utah.

PRAYER LANGUAGE

Print out or photocopy this page. Color and cut apart the five strips. Mix up the strips, then put them back in the appropriate order as you discuss the proper way to pray.

OPENING
OUR FATHER IN HEAVEN
THE LORD JESUS CHRIST COMMANDED, "YE MUST ALWAYS PRAY UNTO THE FATHER IN MY NAME." (3 NEPHI 18:19)

THANKS
WE ARE THANKFUL FOR OUR BLESSINGS
ALWAYS GIVE THANKS TO HEAVENLY FATHER.

ASK
WE ASK THEE TO BLESS US
SEEK HEAVENLY FATHER'S GUIDANCE AND STRENGTH IN ALL YOU DO.

CLOSING
IN THE NAME OF JESUS CHRIST, AMEN
WE SAY "AMEN" TO SHOW THAT WE AGREE WITH THE PRAYER.

RESPECTFUL LANGUAGE
THEE THINE THY THOU
USE THE WORDS ABOVE RATHER THAN YOU, YOUR, AND YOURS.

Prayers Are Answered

Heavenly Father has promised to answer our prayers, just as he answered the prayers of these people from the scriptures.

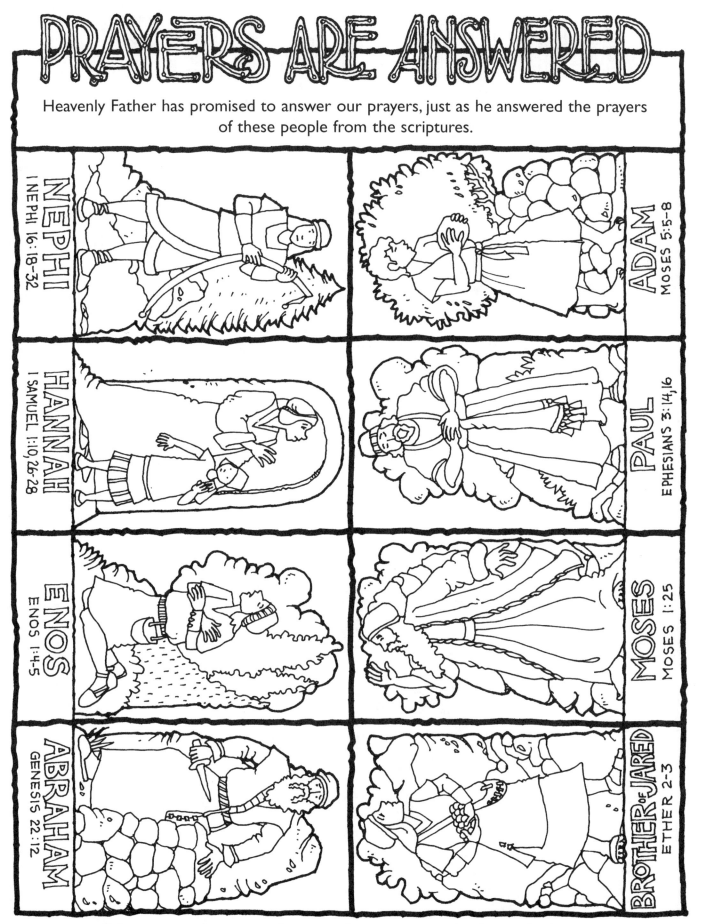

Print out or photocopy the page, then cut out and color each picture.
Look up the scriptures on each picture to learn more about the person depicted.

DANIEL IN THE DEN

Read Daniel 6. Daniel chose to pray even though he was in danger.
Match the five sets of lions.

AUGUST

As I Follow the Direction and Righteous Examples Given in the Scriptures, the Lord Promises Me Rich Blessings

Latter-day prophets counsel us to study the scriptures every day, both individually and with our families. Our church leaders encourage us to "liken" the scriptures to ourselves. We should learn to find ways that the sacred accounts of the past apply to our lives today.

In 1 Nephi 19:24, Nephi states, "Hear ye the words of the prophet, which were written unto all the house of Israel, and liken them unto yourselves, that ye may have hope as well as your brethren from whom ye have been broken off; for after this manner has the prophet written."

The commandments given in the scriptures apply to us today as well as they did to those in the past. One of the reasons we are here on this earth is to show our willingness to our Heavenly Father. By obeying the laws and commandments given, we will be blessed greatly. By reading the scriptures we can learn about the principles of faith, obedience, and repentance. These principles will help us today and in the future.

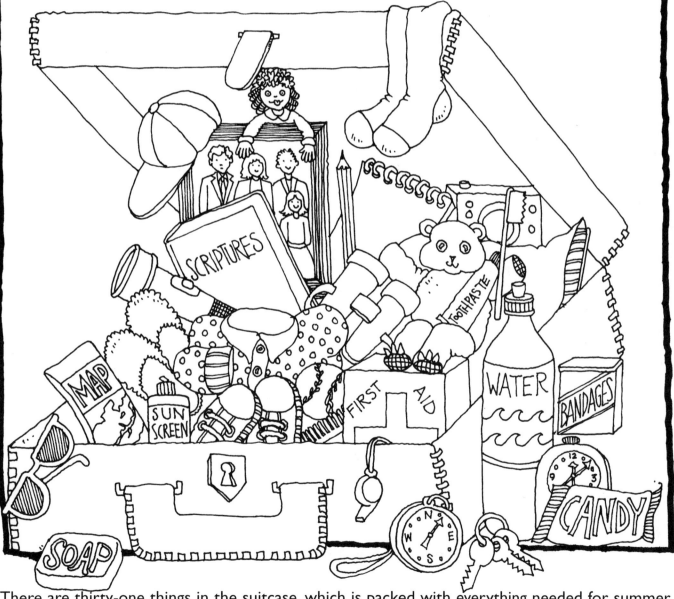

There are thirty-one things in the suitcase, which is packed with everything needed for summer vacation. Read your scriptures every day this month, even if you are on vacation. Color one object for every day you read.

SCRIPTURE

Photocopy or print out these pages. Color and cut out the pictures of the people from the scriptures. Color and cut out the background sections.

NOAH OBEYS

Read Genesis 6–8 to learn about Noah. Then print out or photocopy this page.

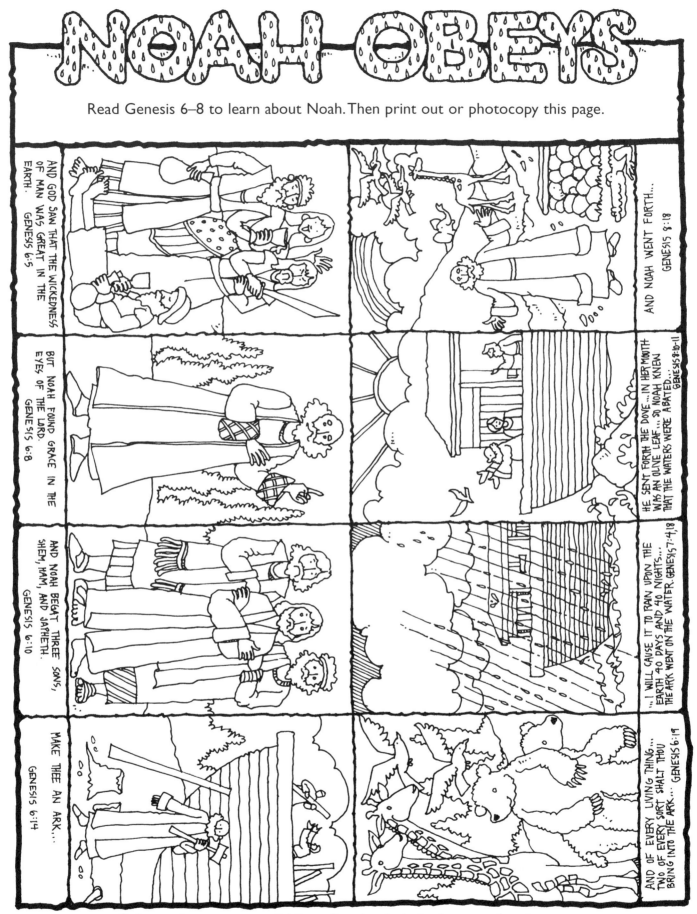

Color and cut out on solid lines. Punch a hole in the top of each square,
then secure them together with a piece of string or a ring to make a flip book.

Steps of Repentance

Kevin has made a bad choice. To repent of his sin he must do five things.

Cross out every other letter in the steps and write the remaining letters in the spaces above to see what he needs to do to feel better. The first letter is crossed out for you.

SEPTEMBER

The Promises Taught in the Scriptures Give Me Comfort and Courage

Even when the world is in turmoil around us, we can receive comfort, courage, and the blessing of inner peace. The words of the Savior teach us how we can experience the peace and comfort the gospel brings. "Peace I leave with you, my peace I give unto you: not as the world giveth, give I unto you. Let not your heart be troubled, neither let it be afraid" (John 14:27).

Many people from the scriptures had to show great courage in their trials and in the oppositions placed before them. When we have faith as they did, we can be guided and receive the courage to overcome evil and obstacles and choose the right. We are counseled to read and study the scriptures each day and be receptive to the whisperings of the Holy Ghost. We are promised that our faith will fortify us against dangers and temptations and we will draw near to our Heavenly Father and his son, Jesus Christ.

It's time to go back to school! Don't forget to read your scriptures every day. Starting at the school bus, color in one square for every day you read your scriptures.

LIAHONA

Connect the dots to see what it was that made the Liahona work.
Read 1 Nephi 16:27–28 when complete.

FAITH WILL GUIDE US

Follow the scriptures about faith to get from one end of the maze to the other. If you come across a statement that does not talk about faith, you are going the wrong way.

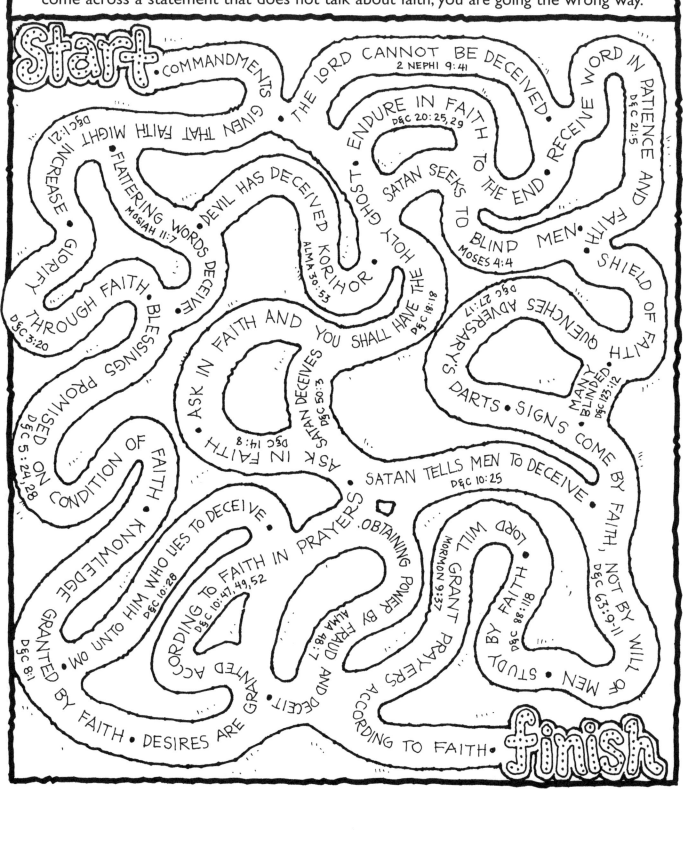

ESTHER'S COURAGE

Queen Esther had the courage to do what was right. Read Esther 2 through 8 to learn her story. Look for the hidden letters E-S-T-H-E-R-S-C-O-U-R-A-G-E.

OCTOBER

Latter-day Prophets Teach Me the Way to Obtain God's Promises

We are blessed to be led by living prophets. These men are inspired and called to speak for the Lord. Prophets testify of Jesus Christ and his gospel. They speak clearly and boldly about avoiding sin and warn us strongly of its consequences. As members of The Church of Jesus Christ of Latter-day Saints, we have a living prophet that we sustain as President of our Church. He is our prophet, seer, and revelator. He is the only person on the earth who receives the revelation to guide our entire church. We also sustain the counselors in the First Presidency and the members of the Quorum of the Twelve Apostles as prophets, seers, and revelators.

If we follow the word of the Lord given through his prophets, we will be blessed with courage, comfort, and help. In general conference, living prophets teach us to choose the right, strengthen our families, and love and serve others.

Color in one numbered area for each day you read the scriptures in October. When you are finished, you will have colored a picture of the Conference Center and Temple Square, filled with people waiting to hear the words of the prophet at general conference.

Prophets Today

Match the words in the numbered boxes with the corresponding empty spaces to learn more about the priesthood and prophets today.

As [6] of the Church of Jesus Christ of Latter-day Saints, we are blessed to be led by [11] — inspired men called to speak for the Lord. We sustain the [18] of the church as our [26] [34] and [8] — the only person on the [29] who [22] revelation to [10] the entire church. We also [20] the [1] in the First Presidency and members of the [19] of the [30] [16] as prophets, [33] and revelators.

The [3] of the church [15] priesthood [27] to other priesthood [7] so they can [25] in their areas of [9] priesthood keys are [12] on presidents of [4] [17] [21] and [23] [28] [13] and quorum presidents.

A priesthood quorum is an organized [5] of [2] who hold the same priesthood office. The primary purposes of quorums are to serve others, build [24] and [31] and instruct one another in doctrines, [32] and [14]

1 COUNSELORS	2 BRETHREN	3 PRESIDENT	4 TEMPLES,	5 GROUP
6 MEMBERS	7 LEADERS	8 REVELATOR	9 RESPONSIBILITY.	10 GUIDE
11 LIVING PROPHETS	12 BESTOWED	13 BRANCH PRESIDENTS,	14 DUTIES.
15 DELEGATES	16 APOSTLES	17 MISSIONS,	18 PRESIDENT	19 QUORUM
20 SUSTAIN	21 STAKES,	22 RECEIVES	23 DISTRICTS,	24 UNITY	25 PRESIDE
26 PROPHET	27 KEYS	28 BISHOPS,	29 EARTH	30 TWELVE	31 BROTHERHOOD
32 PRINCIPLES,	33 SEERS,	34 SEER,

48

CONFERENCE NOTES

As you listen to and watch general conference, color in a space next to the words or subjects on this list each time you hear them. Use different colors to create a pattern.

- Prayer
- Faith
- Jesus Christ
- Family
- Joseph Smith
- Priesthood
- Sacrament
- Holy Ghost
- Heavenly Father
- Baptism
- Agency
- Accountability
- Music
- Happiness
- Eternity
- Conference Center
- Heaven
- Pre-existence
- Prophet
- Apostle
- Bishop
- Aaronic Priesthood
- Melchizedek Priesthood
- Choices
- Mother
- Father
- Book of Mormon
- Pioneers
- Growth
- Trials

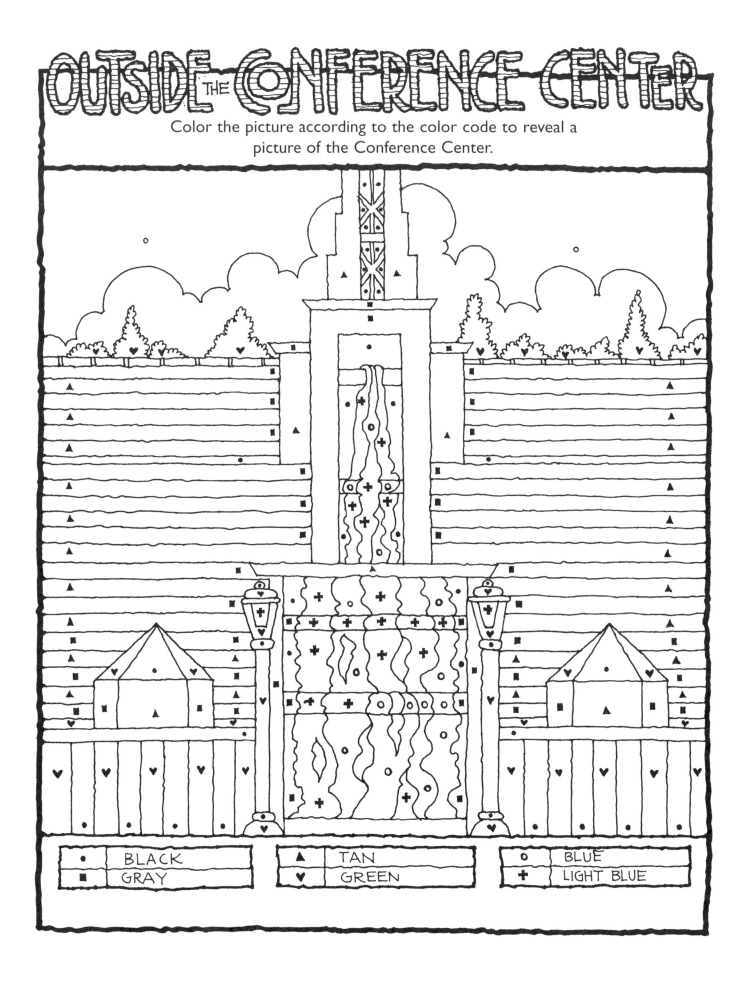

INSIDE THE CONFERENCE CENTER

Color each area marked with a dot to reveal a picture of the place we go to hear general conference.

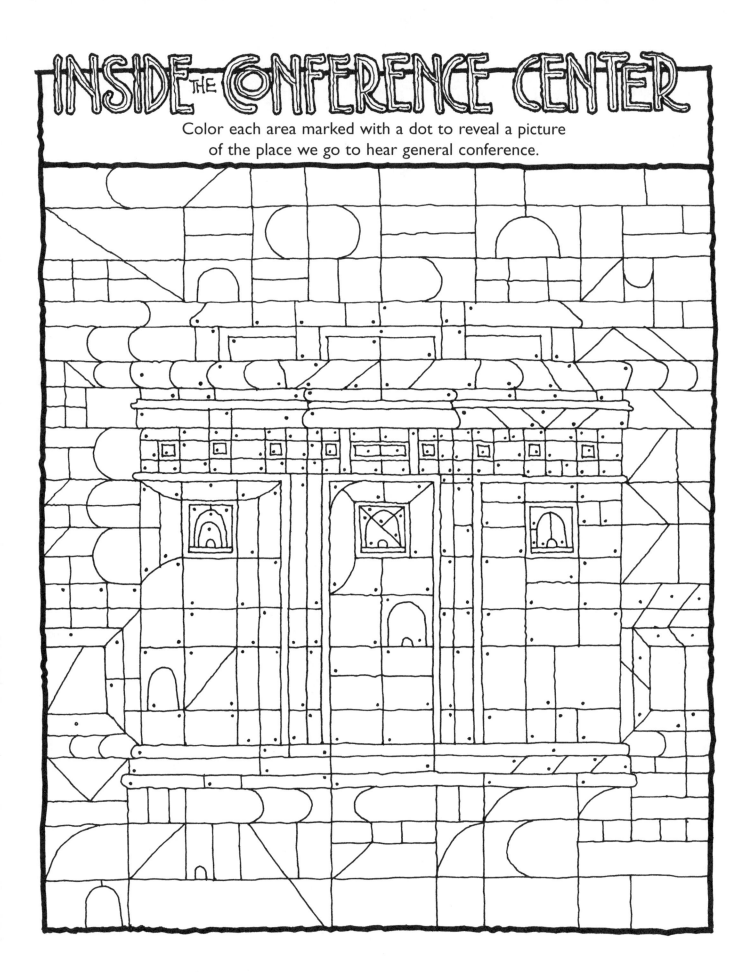

51

NOVEMBER

I Am Thankful for the Promises of Heavenly Father and Jesus Christ—Their Promises Are Sure

Our Father in Heaven has blessed us with everything we have. We need to remember that "he who receiveth all things with thankfulness shall be made glorious" (D&C 78:19). When we work at being grateful and make sure we thank our Father in Heaven for all things, the blessings we receive become obvious and more blessings will be revealed to us.

Heavenly Father has promised us so many things, all depending on our faithfulness. We must always remember to be grateful for his goodness, his commandments, his beloved Son Jesus Christ, and his example.

We should remember to thank him for the Atonement and the restored church. We are always happier when we are grateful and express our thanks, especially to our Father in Heaven.

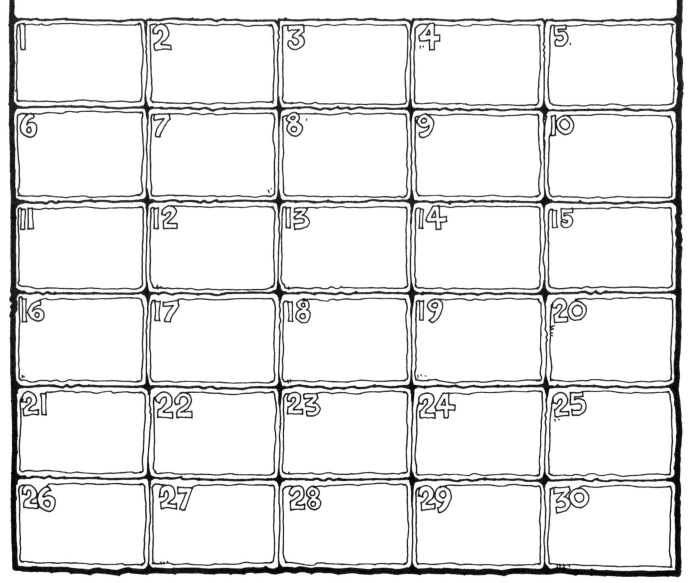

Read your scriptures every day in November. Each day you read, draw a picture of something you are grateful for in the corresponding square. At the end of the month, count your many blessings.

I AM THANKFUL FOR

Print out or photocopy this page. Color the basket and the small pictures. Cut out the basket on the solid lines and fold on the dotted lines. Tape the tabs to the sides.

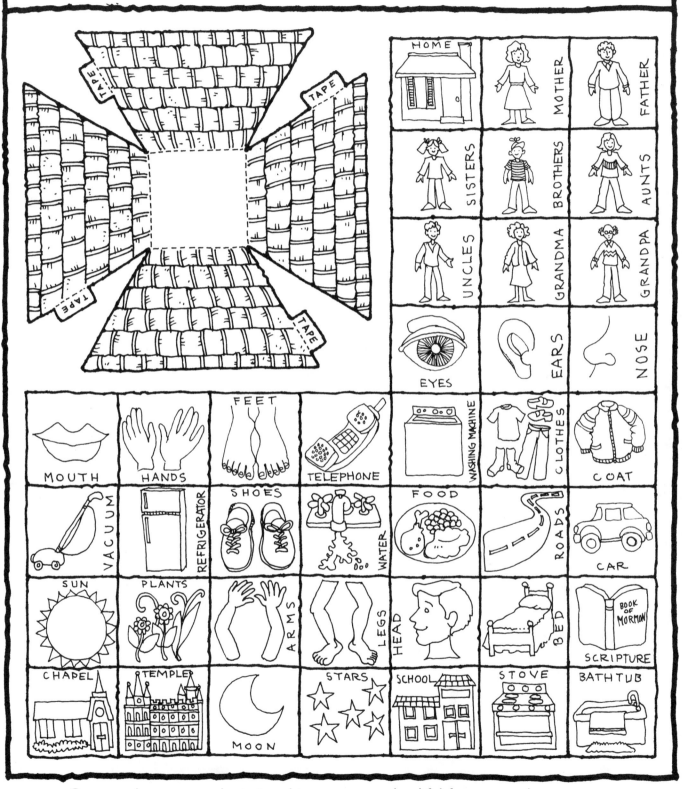

Cut out the squares depicting things you are thankful for—or make your own pictures—and fill up the basket with your blessings.

53

MY GOSPEL

Photocopy or print out these pages. Color and cut out each picture. Punch a hole in the top left-hand corner of each situation and use a

STANDARDS

piece of string or a ring to secure the pages and make a flip book of pictures matching the statements in "My Gospel Standards" on page 30.

BLESSING BINGO

Play bingo using this card and the additional cards on the CD-ROM. Print out the cards, then color and laminate them. Use pennies, buttons, or other small objects as markers to cover up each blessing as it is read. The first person with five markers in a row is the winner. You can also make your own bingo cards by using the blessing squares on page 53. Photocopy, color, and cut them out, then place them in any order you like with glue or tape and photocopy the whole picture to make a new card.

DECEMBER

Heavenly Father Fulfilled His Promise to Send a Savior

Many Old Testament prophets foretold the coming of the Savior. Many Book of Mormon prophets also prophesied of his birth and life. In 1 Nephi 10:4, Lehi prophesied that God would "raise up . . . a Messiah, or, in other words, a Savior of the world." Our Father in Heaven promised, even before the creation of the earth, that he would provide a savior, Jesus Christ, his firstborn son. From our Father in Heaven, Jesus Christ inherited the power to overcome death. From his mortal mother, Mary, he inherited the ability to die. Jesus is the only one to redeem us from our sins. He received this power from Heavenly Father and was able to carry out the Atonement because he kept himself free from sin. Through the Atonement, Jesus redeems all of us from the effects of the Fall, or the spiritual and physical death of Adam and Eve. If we promise to follow Jesus Christ and keep the commandments, our Heavenly Father will keep his promise that we will be happy and live with him again.

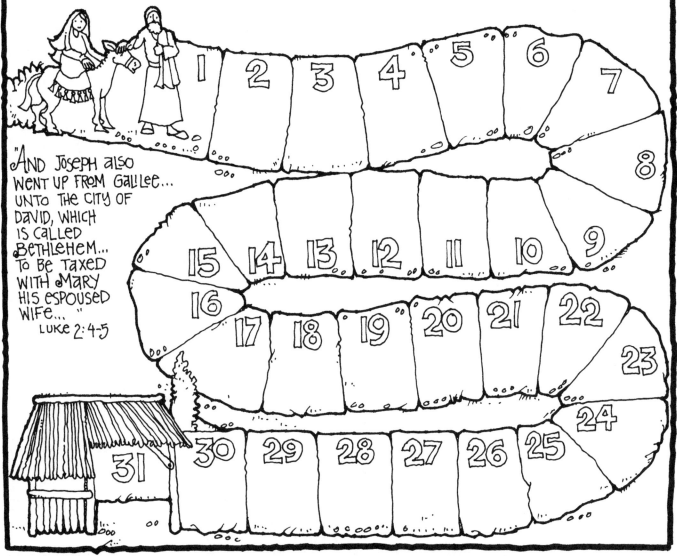

"And Joseph also went up from Galilee... unto the city of David, which is called Bethlehem... to be taxed with Mary his espoused wife..." Luke 2:4-5

Read your scriptures every day in December. Each day you read, color in a section of the road Mary and Joseph took to get to Bethlehem.

ANCIENT PRO

Copy the figures onto cardstock and then color. Cut out the stands with their names and scriptures about them. Fold and connect the stands. Stand the figures in the stands.

LEHI — I NEPHI 10:4-8
KING BENJAMIN — MOSIAH 3:5-8
ABINADI — MOSIAH 16:7-8

PROPHECIES OF CHRIST

Read the scriptures to learn about the prophecies made about the coming of the Savior.

ALMA THE YOUNGER — SAMUEL THE LAMANITE — MORMON

ALMA
ALMA 7:7-13

SAMUEL
HELAMAN 14:2-6

MORMON
MORMON 22-23

59

CHRISTMAS STORY

Color in the Christmas picture according to the colors listed in the box.
Read Luke 2 to learn more about the birth of Jesus.

1	RED	5	TAN
2	BLUE	6	BROWN
3	YELLOW	7	GREEN
4	ORANGE	8	PURPLE

CHRISTMAS GIFTS

Cut out and decorate the Christmas box. Fold where indicated and tape corners together. Color and cut out the special gifts you can give. Put the gifts inside the box.

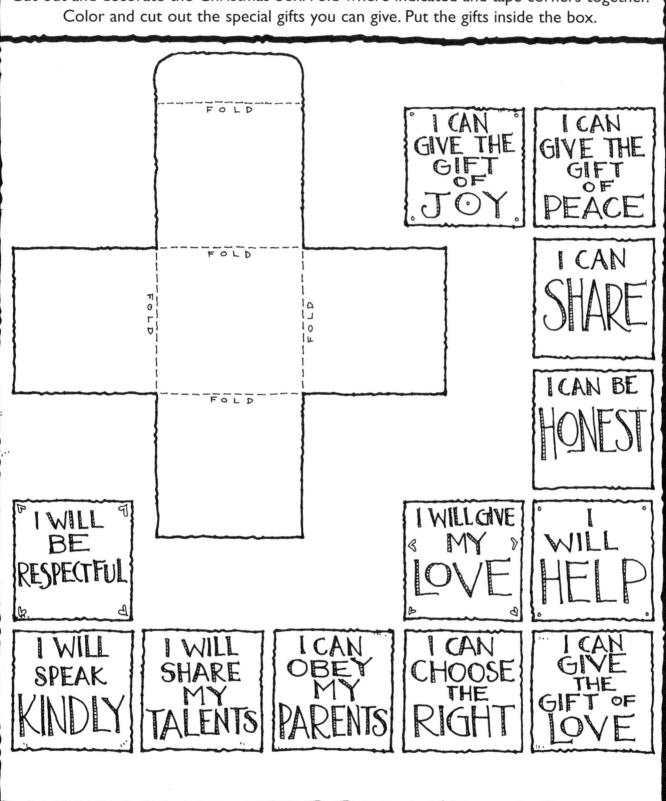

MY TESTIMONY—

NAME DATE